Sir William Wallace

# Tales of Stirling Castle and The Battle of Bannockburn

BY RENNIE McOWAN

Illustrated by
JOHN MACKAY

# INTRODUCTION

A fort has sat a-top of the prominent 250 ft. rock at Stirling for many centuries.

An old saying states that whoever held Stirling, held Scotland.

Dominating a strategic crossing point of the River Forth, the castle at Stirling has played a key role in our Kingdom's history for over 800 years.

Sir William Wallace, Guardian of Scotland, and leader in war, recaptured it from the English in 1297 after the Battle of Stirling Bridge.

King Edward I—the famous Hammer of the Scots—retook it in 1304, and it was regained by King Robert the Bruce in 1314 after the Battle of Bannockburn.

In later centuries it was a favourite residence of the Scottish monarchs.

James II was born there and slew the Earl of Douglas there and both Mary Queen of Scots and James VI lived in the castle.

In the time of James IV a Frenchman, John Damien, dived off the battlements in a bizarre flying experiment.

King James V used to disguise himself as a minor laird—the Gudeman of Ballengeich—and, incognito, travelled around the countryside getting to know the ordinary people.

It was at Stirling, too, that James VI celebrated the baptism of his first son, Prince Henry, by rebuilding the Chapel Royal and by staging a splendid banquet which became the talk of many courts.

The castle in later centuries became a military barracks, and the Great Hall is currently being restored.

The towers built by James III can be seen, and the splendid Renaissance palace of James V, the Parliament Hall, and the Chapel Royal of 1594.

From the battlements the cannon of General Blakeney's Hanoverian garrison fought a gun duel with Bonnie Prince Charlie's Jacobite army.

Nearby is the Heading Hill where James I had some of Scotland's most powerful nobles summarily executed.

In war and peace, the ancient fortress of Stirling is an inseparable part of Scotland's history.

# BATTLE OF STIRLING BRIDGE

Stirling Castle looks to two sites in particular that have prominently figured in battles and power-struggles over the years...Stirling Bridge and the Abbey Craig, which is now topped by the Wallace Monument.

This great tower and viewpoint was erected as a national monument in 1869 to one of Scotland's greatest heroes.

The old stone bridge of Stirling was dominated by the castle and has many a tale to tell of its own. But it was another nearby bridge of wood on stone foundations which was to be the scene of a bloody battle.

No one is precisely certain where this older bridge stood. Some historians say it was at Kildean, others that it was nearer Cambuskenneth Abbey, but no-one denies it was of great strategic importance and—as happened so often—controlled by whoever held the castle.

When the tide is out and the river level falls the remains of wooden piles can be seen, and if these are the actual foundations they mark a watery grave for many a brave knight and many a hardy footsoldier.

The story begins when nearly all of Scotland was under the conquering armies of Edward I of England. The Earl of Surrey was appointed Guardian of Scotland.

Sir Hugh de Cressingham, a Churchman, was treasurer an ensured all the key castles such as Stirling were garrisoned by his own soldiers.

But not all Scots were prepared to accept English rule.

William Wallace was the son of a small landowner, Sir Malcolm Wallace, and he was born at Elderslie, near Paisley.

When he grew up he determined to restore control of Scotland to its own people.

He was tall and strong, and legends of the time say he had fair hair, piercing eyes and a wound-mark on the left-side of his chin.

Wallace began by brawling with soldiers from the garrisons and then serious fighting broke out as resistance grew. It was said that his wife was slain in Lanark during a struggle for possession of the town.

Legend also tells that the Governor of Ayr invited Scottish nobles and other leaders to a meeting and they were then hanged in twos after they had entered the building.

Wallace was invited but was warned in time.

In retaliation, he and his men raided Ayr at night, fastened from the outside the doors of the wooden houses in which the English garrison were billeted and then set them on fire.

More men joined Wallace, and he attacked towns and isolated castles, and gradually began to control much of Scotland.

He was not a great noble, only the son of a minor laird, but his strength, striking appearance, personality and military skill persuaded men of higher rank to serve under his command.

The Earl of Surrey began to fear that Wallace would conquer all of Scotland, and he sent urgent messages to King Edward, asking him to send a large army to crush Wallace.

Over 30,000 knights and footsoldiers were sent north to Stirling. Wallace heard the news when he was beseiging Dundee; the only town north of the Tay still in English hands, and he quickly broke off the siege.

He planned to halt the English army at the inevitable strategic point of Stirling.

By forced marches he speedily got his army of 10,000 to Stirling and took up position on the Abbey Craig, hiding most of his men among the trees.

He had excellent observation over the lower ground and could see the English soldiers gathering together on the south side of the river.

Wallace knew that the wooden bridge across the Forth was so narrow that it could only take columns of men and horses if they marched two abreast.

He could not really believe the English commanders would permit their army to cross, thus dividing it into two halves, but he hoped against hope that they would.

There was a ford nearby, suitable when the tide was out.

The Earl of Surrey was an experienced soldier and did not want the army to cross over the bridge and attack the strongly placed Scots, but Cressingham is said to have contemptuously insisted on speed and to have been certain of victory.

Wallace watched the oncoming horsemen with baited breath and great satisfaction, and gave instructions to his troops to get ready for instant action.

A very brave Knight, Sir Marmaduke de Twenge, who was Keeper of Stirling Castle, led the English heavy cavalry across the bridge, and they were then followed by other horsemen and

*'Very few survived on the North side of the river'*

footsoldiers of a division commanded by Cressingham.

Because of the narrowness of the bridge the pace was slow. It was midday before about one-half of the English army reached the north bank of the Forth and fanned out in a defensive bridgehead.

Then Wallace struck!

A large group of Scots spearmen made as if to go to the river bank to block the English advance, and then they suddenly changed direction. They formed a tight wedge of levelled spears and charged at the portion of the English column just leaving the bridge.

They crashed into the ill-prepared soldiers, dislodged them and occupied one end of the bridge.

Then, back to back, fighting fiercely, they held off the hampered English troops on the bridge who could only come at them two at a time, and at the same time they beat off counter-attacks from the troops on the north bank who realised the Scots now had control of the bridge and had cut their army in half. Marmaduke de Twenge refused to follow some of his men who leaped into the waters of the Forth and tried to swim across, and he managed to cut his way back on to the bridge and rejoin his comrades.

But, after that, the Scots kept the bridge-end firmly closed.

Wallace, timing his main charge to perfection, sent his army crashing into the English horsemen, driving them back on Cressingham's men.

Surrey and the men of the stranded other half of his army watched in bitter anger, and helpless, as the long spears of the Scots drove both footsoldiers and cavalry back in disorder, until they poured over the river-banks and into the waters of the Forth.

Thousands perished on the banks or were drowned.

The Earl of Surrey bravely tried to force his way over the bridge, but was blocked by corpses, wounded men, maimed horses kicking out and screaming, and the on-coming rush of the Scots.

Very few survived on the north side of the river and there was further consternation when part of the bridge collapsed and fell into the water.

Some reports of the time say Wallace had the bridge undermined so that when key pins were driven out it fell into the Forth, but others say the bridge gave way under the weight of the fighting.

Whatever the reason, the collapsed bridge helped the Scots who had nearly all of their army on the Abbey Craig side, and it spelled doom for the now-surrounded bridgehead who could not be reinforced.

Cressingham was among the many slain: his corpse had a spear driven through it.

Wallace followed up the carnage by ordering his men to cross at the ford at Kildean and to pursue Surrey's division.

The Earl eventually retreated to Berwick, and returned to England.

The remnants of the English army were later attacked by another Scots force at Torwood, stationed by Wallace to be ready for just such an eventuality, and here again casualties were heavy.

The victory was complete.

Ahead of Wallace lay further victories, the freeing of his country, the re-establishment of Scottish trade with the Continent and raids into England.

Also ahead of him lay eventual defeat at the Battle of Falkirk, betrayal to King Edward, and a cruel execution in London.

His head was placed on a pole at London Bridge and other parts of his corpse were sent to Newcastle, Berwick, Stirling and Perth as a warning to others.

But the fires that Wallace kindled were not put out and were eventually to burn again under King Robert the Bruce.

The Wallace Monument dominates the area around Stirling, the river which was part of his plan and the ancient castle which he took after his overwhelming victory at Stirling Bridge.

# FOR SCOTLAND'S FREEDOM

King Robert the Bruce was very angry. His brother, Sir Edward, had made a pledge that might well ruin all he had planned and struggled for over so many years.

The King of the Scots had been fighting guerilla actions against the English armies in Scotland since he was crowned at Scone in March 1306. His reign had not begun well.

His small army had been quickly defeated and scattered. His friends were hanged, or fled into hiding. His relatives were imprisoned and cruelly treated.

His estates were forfeited.

But still he had continued the fight, determined to succeed and to restore Scotland's independence.

He spent the winter abroad, returned to Scotland in 1307 and waged unceasing war against the English, and the Scots who supported them and who did not agree with Bruce's claim to be King.

He knew he could not yet win a pitched battle. He did not have enough men or a secure base.

But he had outstanding commanders, tested in many a skirmish and ambush, and he made skilful use of the Scottish forests, and of lonely glens and mountains, to hide his small band.

He found isolated garrisons of English soldiers, and the Scots who aided them, and demolished them.

He defeated sizeable English forces on ground of his own choosing. He captured strong-points and towns, sacked and burned the buildings, destroyed weapons, food and stores and then melted back into the countryside.

It was the classic guerilla-pattern that we have seen so often in modern times, during the Second World War and afterwards.

By keeping rigidly to this pattern, he gradually began to drive the English forces back into the main castles and keeps.

Many Scots flocked to join his standard.

He totally crushed the powerful Comyn family who did not want Bruce as king, and he was then free to turn his whole attention to the English forces.

Gradually, the leading Scottish towns and castles fell to him.

An exception was Stirling Castle, strong and dominating, controlling all traffic north and south and the narrow waistland of Scotland. It had an unrivalled strategic importance. It was said of Stirling that it was a brooch that clasped Highlands and Lowlands together.

Sir Edward Bruce had laid seige the castle and after three months he had a parley with the castle commander, Sir Philip Mowbray.

The commander said he would surrender if an English army failed to appear within three leagues of the castle by Midsummer's Day 1314.

Edward Bruce impetuously agreed, perhaps carried away by the steady flow of Scottish successes. He had always been a man of action, and indeed it was he who had encouraged Bruce to persevere in the struggle when they had re-landed on the Scottish mainland.

When King Robert was told he was deeply displeased.

He knew that the pledge meant that the English now had a chance to meet the Scots in pitched battle, an event he had deliberately avoided.

Bruce was not sure his men were ready. He knew that the English could put a huge army of armoured knights into the field, and that they could produce many archers who had been the decisive element in other battles.

It was the archers who had defeated Wallace at the Battle of Falkirk in 1298, the hail of arrows breaking the schiltron, the ring, of Scottish spearmen, thus opening up gaps and leaving them prey to the charge of knights on heavy horses.

Bruce's hit-and-hide tactics had been successful. Now the pattern was to change and he was uneasy.

But the deed was done, and the pledge had been made.

Stirling Castle, which had proved a stumbling block for many armies, was to be the price for the victor of one of the greatest conflicts of the Scottish Wars of Independence.

King Edward II of England was not the iron-hard soldier his father had been, the famous "Hammer of the Scots", but he was still determined to accept the challenge from this upstart Scot.

He was certain that if he could defeat the Scots in pitched battle he could win all back that he had lost in Scotland since Bruce was crowned and either rule himself or instal a puppet King.

He gathered a huge army of 25,000 foot soldiers armed with spears, axes and swords. He also recruited many Welsh archers, armed with longbows.

He had over 2,000 heavy cavalry, and they were expected to

crush the Scots troops in the same way as modern tanks could over-run infantrymen.

King Edward also had the help of some Scots, such as the Comyns, MacDougalls and MacNabs, who opposed Bruce.

It was a vast army for the time, with a supply and baggage train of over 200 wagons.

So confident was King Edward and his commanders of an easy victory, that in addition to food, spare arms, equipment and pay for the troops, they carried furniture and other goods for some of the nobles who were to be given Scottish estates once the expected crushing victory had taken place.

But Bruce held many cards. His army, although small, was well-disciplined, accustomed to command, lean and experienced, and had been together as a close-knit fighting unit for some years.

He had about 7,000 soldiers, but only a few hundred cavalry-men, mounted on light horses.

Bruce had two months to bring his army to readiness for a pitched battle.

He obviously had to prevent the relief of Stirling Castle, and he had also to try to destroy King Edward's army.

He was determined not to repeat the mistakes of the battle of Falkirk, and trained his men to become proficient in quickly forming the Scottish battle ring, the schiltron. He also taught them to "break hedgehog" and to counter-attack in formation, a device intended to overcome the problem of immobility shown at Falkirk. His men had 12 ft. spears, swords, axes and dirks, protective helmets, mail gloves to hold the spears, and padded coats to stop arrows.

In defence the schiltron formed an unbroken wall of spears against the charge of the armoured knights. In advance, it relied on numbers to add weight and to press home the attack with levelled spears.

Practice and discipline were essential and Bruce saw that his men had these.

He split his force into four divisions, under battle-tried commanders.

The first was commanded by Randolph, Earl of Moray, who had captured Edinburgh Castle in a daring raid the year before. The second division was led by Sir Edward Bruce, no doubt pensive about what his rash promise to the commander of the castle had brought. The third was led by the feared Sir James Douglas.

Next to Bruce, Douglas was the greatest hero among the Scots. Because of his dark complexion he was called the "Black Douglas".

He became such a terror to the invaders that mothers used to repeat a rhyme to their children:

"Hush thee, hush thee, do not fret thee,
The Black Douglas will not get thee!"

It was Douglas who had planned the famous capture of his own castle of Douglasdale, in Lanarkshire. When the English garrison had attended church on Palm Sunday, Douglas' men were in the congregation with weapons below their cloaks. At a signal from Douglas, who dropped his cloak and shouted "A Douglas! A Douglas!" they fell upon the garrison. All were killed. Then they took the castle, replenished their own stores, and made a great heap of casks, foodstuffs, and corpses and set fire to it all. This famous raid was known as the Douglas Larder.

The King commanded the fourth, the strongest division.

Bruce was also aided by about 2,000 "small folk", the ordinary people who had lost homes and families and who wanted to join in the fray. They were poorly armed and ill-disciplined, but legend has it that they were to play a key part in the battle.

The cavalry, under Sir Alexander Keith, were to be kept for a special role.

There were men from nearly all parts of Scotland in the King's army, from Ross and Moray, from towns like Inverness, Elgin and Nairn, from areas like Buchan, Mar, Angus, Strathearn, Menteith and Lennox. There were men from central Scotland and from the Borders.

The King's own division had Macdonalds from the west, from Kintyre and Argyll, and men from his own area of Carrick, Kyle and Cunningham.

It was a truly national army with many Clans taking part, including Camerons, Campbells, Frasers, Gordons, Macphersons, Macleans, MacGregors, Mackenzies, Ross' and Sinclairs.

The king set up his supply base at Cambuskenneth, in the loop of the Forth, not far from the castle.

On the 17th of June the English army left its southern bases and marched to Edinburgh. On the 22nd they left Edinburgh for Falkirk.

The next morning they set out for Stirling along the line of the old Roman road. They still had two days in which to relieve the castle which could be clearly seen and which drew all eyes.

To start with Bruce kept his strongest division as a rearguard at the Torwood, between Stirling and Falkirk, with horse-patrols keeping an eye on the enemy. His main troops busied themselves preparing defensive positions covering Stirling.

They made skilful use of the line of the Bannockburn, and of the marshes and bogs which were then plentiful. He ordered pits to be dug, with spikes called calthrops placed inside, and for the pits to be covered so that they would maim the horses and the charging English knights.

His main position was a good one just inside the line of the New Park, between the Borestone and Bannockburn. His right wing was partly hidden in scrub and forest and his left along an escarpment which gave him good observation.

His plan would force King Edward to attack from the front over difficult ground for horses or to risk going round the left flank over other difficult terrain.

If King Edward were to take the left flank, Bruce thought it might present a good opportunity to attack.

Later Bruce withdrew his division from the Torwood into his main position, to hold the edge of the wood in the New Park. He kept horse patrols out in front.

Edward Bruce's men held the high ground to the left. Moray was stationed near St. Ninian's Church to watch the flat ground of the Carse. The rest were kept in the Borestone area (near the present Rotunda site). Tradition has it that the present Rotunda site where the Bruce statue is situated was Bruce's command post during part of the battle.

The ill-disciplined small-folk, panting to get at the enemy, were stationed behind Coxet Hill.

From the battlements of the castle, the anxious defenders peered, watching the sun glint on spears and armour, seeing clouds of dust and flags and pennants, and tried to unravel what the manoeuverings might mean, and whether they would be dead or alive in the next day or two.

They now knew with certainty that one of Scotland's greatest battles was about to take place.

*Robert the Bruce ~ King of Scots*

# VICTORY AT BANNOCKBURN

The main body of the defenders of Stirling Castle joined their sentries on the battlements at first light on June 23, 1314 but they could discern little amid the trees and bogs.

Then they saw what appeared to be several hundred knights riding along the edge of the carse as if they were trying to get between the Scots army and the castle.

King Edward had ordered them to take up a position where they could harass the Scots once he had carried out his plan to dislodge them with a mammoth frontal assault.

Meanwhile, the van of the main body of cavalry, foot and archers led by the Earl of Hereford and the Earl of Gloucester, moved slowly towards the Scots. Bruce, unarmoured and mounted on a light pony, inspected his forward troops while still keeping a wary eye on the enemy. He accidentally strayed too far from his own lines.

One of the English knights, Sir Henry de Bohun, recognised the King by the coronet he was wearing on his helmet and suddenly left his own men and charged towards him. Bruce's commanders watched helplessly. They were too far away to go to his aid. Then alarm changed to exaltation. Bruce waited until the lance point was almost at his chest, then quickly wheeled the pony, dodged the lance, and split de Bohun's helmet and skull with his light battle-axe. A great cheer went up from the Scots troops.

On being reproved by his commanders for risking his life so near to the fighting, he merely remarked: "Alas, I have broken my good battle-axe".

The elated Scots troops charged the English advance guards and drove them back against the main body.

Horses screamed and reared as they stepped on the pointed calthrops in the pits. Many others were deliberately lanced or hacked by the Scots to bring down their armoured riders.

The dust rose and fell and, when it cleared, the castle defenders saw the van of the English army falling back.

The Scots, under the tight control of the king, held their positions in the wood of the New Park and were greatly heartened by their initial success.

Meanwhile, the English force under Clifford and de Bowmont, sent along the edge of the carse, had not been seen by Moray's division, whose duty it was to guard that side. He was reprimanded by Bruce who sent messengers to warn him. "A rose has fallen from your chaplet", he said.

The stung Moray hurried his schiltrons down to the low ground. The Scots' careful training began to prove itself as they moved quickly in disciplined bodies, spears at the ready.

The English knights then charged the on-coming Scots who formed a dour and resolute hedgehog, and a desperate fight took place.

Knights flung maces and axes into the Scots ring, trying to force an opening so that they could use the weight of their horses, but the sweating spearsmen held firm.

Douglas became anxious about his hard-pressed comrades, but the king told him to hold his own position and not to go to Moray's aid.

Then the Scots got their second wind, and as the English knights withdrew slightly they quickly broke the ring, formed their attack-formation and moved forward with their long spears ready to strike.

The castle defenders, trying to make sense of the affray, suddenly saw the English force break up, one half galloping back to the main body, the other heading for the castle. The gates were quickly opened, and the English cavalry clattered in, many of the horses with spear wounds and some carrying wounded men slumped over the horses' heads or grimly clinging to the reins.

They joined the defenders of the castle they had so eagerly hoped to relieve.

The Scots were pleased with themselves, and their success in these probing skirmishes.

They had shown that their footsoldiers could beat off an attack by charging knights, and that their often-practised drills were effective in all-out war. They had killed Clifford, one of the commanders of the cavalry force.

They had broken up and dislodged the force of knights King Edward had sent to place themselves strategically to the Scots rear, ready to strike when the moment was right.

And they had blocked the advance of the van of the English army and had sent it reeling back.

The opening phases of the battle had gone the Scots way.

Bruce's success in single combat had also been a great morale

*'Pits with spikes to maim the English'*

booster.

King Edward called an urgent council of war. His angry commanders pointed out that they could only dislodge the Scots from the New Park trees and scrub with great difficulty because the position was such a strong one.

They could not easily work round to the right in an out-flanking movement because of the nature of the terrain.

The English soldiers were tired because of their long, forced marches to try and get to Stirling by the pledged date.

In the middle of all the heated talking and debate, the flaps of the headquarters tent parted and a man in a dark cloak entered. It was Sir Philip Mowbray, the commander of the castle. He had sneaked out, evaded the Scots sentries, and now insisted to King Edward that the castle was now technically relieved.

But King Edward, angered by the day's reverses, wanted victory. He also needed larger supplies of drinking water for his huge numbers of men and horses, so he decided to move nearer to Stirling.

He planned to cross the Bannockburn and move towards the Forth, and relieve the castle the next day.

King Edward was sure that Bruce, with his much smaller army, would not leave his prepared positions and attack him.

But Bruce was a superb tactician, and knew his ground. He knew that the carse ground was low-lying, rough, cut by the Bannockburn and the Pelstream, and by ditches and pools.

At that time the banks of these burns were steep and the bottom soft and muddy. There were many bogs, and part of the Bannockburn was tidal where it joined the Forth.

King Edward moved into this rough territory to get to drier ground and his weary troops bivouacked for the night. It took a long time to transfer such large numbers of men to the drier ground, and reports say the wagons could not be moved and the troops had no food.

The English soldiers slept badly, and there were false alarms because the sentries were edgy about the possibility of a Scots night attack.

Bruce had considered breaking off the battle, taking his men into the hills of the west and continuing his guerilla warfare.

But a Scots knight who had been in King Edward's army deserted and told Bruce that English morale was low and that their position in the carse was uncomfortable and disorganised.

Bruce now knew that because of the nature of the ground, the English army could not easily manoeuvre, and that the cavalry would be hampered. This would greatly reduce the English

'The Scottish Spearmen

*kept up the pressure'*

superiority in numbers.

He decided to attack them across the carse with Edward Bruce's division on the right, then Moray and Douglas, each slightly back to the left. His own division would be the reserve. The small folk were moved to the edge of the escarpment as a further reserve but possibly just to keep them out of the way.

With such limited ground for movement an ill-disciplined mob could be a major hindrance.

The few Scottish horsemen were kept well hidden.

June 24 was a sunny day, and the castle defenders, still keeping their anxious vigil, saw the Scots move down from their strong positions on to the flat ground.

It was St. John's Day, and the army attended Mass said by their chaplains.

They knelt in prayer, almost within bow shot of the English army.

Reports say that King Edward exclaimed: "They kneel for mercy!" But an English knight replied: "Yes, sire, but not from you—they mean to attack".

Quickly, King Edward ordered his knights to saddle and his bowmen drove off the few Scottish archers who were out in front of their advancing spearmen.

The Earl of Gloucester commanded the van of the main English body, and he ordered a charge. Edward Bruce's men skilfully and doggedly formed a hedgehog, and the charge perished in a welter of whinnying horses, broken spears, the screams and shouts of wounded and dying men. Gloucester was killed by the Scots spearmen, and the charge was halted.

Moray's division came storming up on the left and crashed into the English van. It broke and fell back on the main body.

The main armies now clanged together in a melee of hacking, swearing, shouting men, and the archers on both sides could not fire for fear of hitting their own comrades.

Douglas's men, too, pushed forward in formation until the three Scottish divisions were all engaged in hectic hand-to-hand combat.

The Scots were inferior in numbers, but the narrowness of the front prevented the English army from widening out. The water obstacles, the broken ground, the steady pressure from the front, began to cause chaos. Orders were not passed. Men became confused. Those at the front were fiercely engaged. Those behind, pressed in mass, could not reach their enemy, nor manoeuvre.

The Scottish spearmen kept up the pressure. Their experience and training told, and as they were getting the necessary weight to press home their attack, the long spears caused havoc.

But the English army, which contained many brave and skilled soldiers, managed to get a body of archers out on the Scots left, and a hail of arrows began to open up gaps in the Scottish ranks.

For a moment it looked as if it was to be like the battle of Falkirk all over again, but Bruce sent an urgent message to Keith to charge with his few horsemen.

The Scottish cavalry, small in number, had been anxiously watching the fighting, and given their chance, they charged the archers, scattered them and drove them from the field.

A dangerous moment had passed, and the Scots attack regained its momentum.

Bruce now turned to the Macdonalds and the men of the Western Isles in his own and strongest division. To their chief, Angus Og, he gave orders for them to attack and said: "My hope is constant in thee!"

This saying later became the motto of Clanranald, and the Macdonalds' behaviour at Bannockburn was to give them the automatic and proud place of right-of-the-line in Royal armies. (When they did not get it at Culloden, during the Jacobite Rising of 1745 they were so resentful that they did not fight with their normal resolution).

Bruce's timing was just right. His division charged into the press of men, and the English lines began to give ground under the renewed pressure.

The Scots scented victory, and the lines of spearmen began to press the main army back on those behind who could not help them because of the narrow front. The archers in the rear of the English army were out of effective range, and could not be called on in any meaningful way.

"On them, on them, they fail, they fail," shouted the Scots.

Then came an incident which has now passed into legend.

The small folk, the farmers, peasants, fishermen, the workmen, herders and huntsmen, with improvised weapons and no discipline, but who had been held in reserve on the escarpment, could stand the sight no more and poured over the edge.

They pelted towards the fighting armies.

At the sight of what they took to be further Scottish reserves, the main mass of the English army gave way.

A disorganised retreat and near-massacre began.

King Edward was persuaded the day was lost, and retreated to Stirling Castle.

One of his bravest knights, Sir Giles d'Argentine, who had been ordered to look after the king, saw him near to the castle and then said: "I am not accustomed to flee, nor am I going to begin now".

He returned to the battle, charged into the cheering on-coming Scots, and was killed.

The main mass of the English army broke towards the Forth. Many perished in the steep gorge of the Bannockburn. Others drowned in the pools and marshes and mud. In places men could walk on dead horses and corpses, forming a grisly bridge.

The English supply train was captured, valued at today's prices in the region of five to seven million pounds.

English casualties were colossal. Nearly all archers and foot-soldiers being killed or captured, and many nobles and knights killed, or taken prisoner or held to ransom.

The slaughter went on for miles.

The Scots had suffered as well, particularly in the early fighting, but for them it was an overwhelming victory.

At the castle the demoralised garrison again opened the gates to let in a large contingent of fleeing English horsemen.

Sir Philip Mowbray refused to permit King Edward to enter as he felt honour bound to surrender the castle.

The king escaped to Dunbar. A small boat took him to Berwick and England, and as the song says, "to think again".

The next day the victorious Scots re-mustered at the castle, and the garrison surrendered.

Edward Bruce's rash promise had turned out successfully, and Stirling Castle—the main strategic fortress of Scotland—and the focal point of the battle was once again in the hands of the Scots in their quest for independence.

# MURDER AND INTRIGUE

One of the problems for a king long ago was that he had to struggle against powerful nobles. He often had to uneasily look over his shoulder, to play one faction against the other, to keep the balance of power, and yet to maintain his over-all position as sovereign.

It wasn't easy, and many a man ended his life in the dungeons or on the gallows or block because he strayed too far and incurred either the king's anger or the ire of one of the great families.

King James II had a red mark on his face, and was known as "Fiery Face". He also had a fiery temper, and the defiance of some of his nobles sometimes produced outbursts of a terrible anger.

He was determined to bring peace to his troubled realm and he re-enacted some of the laws from his father's reign, and he added some others. He issued proclamations for keeping the peace, and penalties for rebellion and treason.

James wanted to show he was going to be firm, and he was uneasy about the growing power of the Douglases and other leading families. He had good reason for as a young boy he had been a pawn in the hands of the great nobles.

It could not be said that King James II had a pleasant start to life: his father had been murdered by the Grahams in Blackfriars Monastery in Perth when he was only six.

He could not be crowned at Scone, the usual place for Scottish Kings, because of fears for his safety. Instead the ceremony was performed in the chapel at Holyrood Palace.

His mother was virtually a prisoner of Sir William Crichton, governor of Edinburgh Castle, but the queen managed to outwit him and get herself and the young King to Stirling Castle.

She asked leave to go on pilgrimage to a particular church to pray for her son: she was permitted to take two boxes for her luggage. The queen put James in one box and her luggage in the other, and fled to Stirling.

'The Queen hid James in a box'

Even there, he was in peril.

Sir Alexander Livingstone was governor at Stirling and he, like Sir William Crichton, sought to be the leading man in the Kingdom.

The queen was told that both she and the boy-King must do as they were told, even although Archibald, Earl of Douglas, had been nominally appointed the King's lieutenant.

(This particular member of the renowned and feared Douglas family turned out to be weak and indecisive).

The two ambitious castle governors then pretended to be friends and planned to divide power between them but their private pact broke up.

Sir William Crichton, at Edinburgh, schemed to get direct control of the King once again.

He knew that James went hunting near Stirling Castle and he had him watched and his movements timed and noted.

Then, one night, he hid himself and his men in the bushes and when morning came and the King went out with only a few attendants he found himself surrounded by armed men.

The young King was told that he was to return to Edinburgh Castle for his own protection.

The self-seeking planning of the nobles went on, and the two castle governors made yet another pact with one another. This time their new enemy was William, Earl of Douglas, who had succeeded the King's lieutenant to the huge Douglas estates.

The governors feared Douglas power, and it was therefore in their own interests to temporarily join up and oppose or kill him. Doubtless, each had plans to deal with the other once Douglas was out of the way.

The young King James was then forced to preside over an infamous deed of treachery, and perhaps it was that which made him act as he did at Stirling Castle many years later.

William, Earl of Douglas, was 18, vigorous and bold, when he, his brother David (his heir) and another relative were invited to Edinburgh Castle, probably in the King's name. When they got there they were hospitably received.

The Douglases were uneasy as there seemed to be a great many Crichton and Livingstone retainers around, but they were re-assured by the behaviour of the young boy-King who appeared to be enjoying their company and who was unaware of the nobles' plot.

Then Sir William Crichton and Sir Alexander Livingstone accused Earl Douglas of being a traitor, and legend has it that a bull's head was placed on the table during the meal.

This was a sign for the governors' men to seize the Douglases and to bind them.

Young King James protested and wept at the arrest of these friendly guests, but he was forced to preside at a mock trial after which the Douglases were quickly beheaded.

But the Douglases were not finished, and they were to ultimately prove a sore trial to James II.

The estates eventually came to another Earl William, who was to be one of the greatest and most notorious leaders of that belligerent family.

Earl William sided with Livingstone against Crichton, and the nation of Scotland was plagued by power struggles, plundering, internal war and lawlessness.

The situation worsened. Bishop James Kennedy of St. Andrews, a nephew of James I, feared that the Douglases would become so powerful that they would equal or replace the King. So he teamed up with Sir William Crichton. The strife spread as the powerful Earl of Crawford joined Douglas and laid waste the bishop's diocese. The bishop excommunicated the Earl, who did not seem unduly perturbed, but who later died in a skirmish. So the strife went on.

Young King James—lucky to survive—married Mary of Gueldres, in Holland, when he was 19 and set out to put his country to rights, and to curb the power of the great families.

Suddenly, he jailed all the leading members of the Livingstone family, took their lands and arranged a trial. The father was kept in prison and the sons were executed.

Then he turned his attention to the Douglases.

They had mammoth estates in central and southern Scotland. They could muster armies almost as large as the King's.

Earl William had two brothers who were also earls. All were experienced in war against the English, and collectively they were among the most powerful factions in the land.

An old saying stated that no one dared touch a Douglas or a Douglas man.

But the King was astute.

His spies told him that Earl William had made a secret alliance with the Earl of Ross and the new—and notoriously cruel—Earl of Crawford.

King James had already shown the Douglas that he was not to be trifled with for when the Earl was abroad the King had attacked and taken Douglas Craig, one of the earl's castles. He beseiged others, and forced Douglas' men to swear loyalty to the crown.

When the Earl returned, he felt it wise to bow for the moment to the King. James, perhaps thinking of the terrible bull's head dinner so many years ago, relented and returned Douglas' estates in the hope that this reconciliation would bring peace.

Then the King heard that Douglas had begun to intrigue with the English, and he was greatly angered.

The King was also infuriated by an incident when the nephew of Sir Patrick Gray, captain of the King's Guard, was imprisoned by Douglas because he had refused to join Douglas in his wild affrays and his defiance of the King's laws.

The King sent Sir Patrick to Threave Castle to ask for his release.

The Earl received Sir Patrick civilly, and quoted an old proverb about its being ill talking between a full man and fasting, and refused to discuss any business until Sir Patrick had eaten.

Douglas then read the King's letter. Douglas said that the prisoner, MacLellan, the tutor of the young laird of Bombie, would be put at Sir Patrick's disposal.

He then presented him with MacLellan—minus his head which had been removed during lunch.

Sir Patrick calmly withdrew, but once outside the gates he flung his gauntlet at the castle walls, cursed Douglas, and rode for his life.

Douglas also infuriated James by; 1, Holding his own parliament and forbidding people to attend the official one; 2, A flow of high-handed actions, including the murder and hanging of the King's friends.

The King, his patience sorely tried, invited Douglas to Stirling Castle and promised him safe conduct in a letter under the privy seal.

Douglas came with only a handful of attendants on February 21, 1452.

He was received well and entertained to dinner and supper on the following day.

After supper, about seven o'clock in the evening, the king led him to an inner chamber. He decided to have it out, as we would say nowadays, and he challenged Douglas about the bond between himself and the Earls of Crawford and Ross.

Douglas refused all questions. The discussion grew heated. They were both young men: the King was 21, Douglas 26, and they had the impatience of youth as well as living in a violent age. The King demanded answers.

Douglas still refused to answer.

Perhaps he felt secure in the knowledge of safe conduct, and once he was back on his own lands he could muster almost as many men as the king.

Tempers flared, and the king—his fiery temper now at boiling point and with all thought of safe conduct gone—drew a knife.

He shouted: "False traitor, if you will not break the bond, I shall!"

He plunged his knife twice into Earl William's body.

Hearing the uproar, Sir Patrick Gray, Sir Alexander Boyd, Stewart of Darnley and other courtiers rushed in. Sir Patrick, the same man whose nephew had been murdered by Douglas and who had flung his gauntlet at the walls of Threave Castle, struck him with a pike. The others also stabbed Earl William, and his body was hurled out of a window.

There was consternation in the land when the news spread.

Many thought the king had blundered, to slay without a trial. He had broken his word, rumour said. People were scandalised: the king was well liked by the common people. He would go among them, was accessible to them, and at times shared the rations and the quarters of the ordinary soldiers.

James Douglas, brother of the murdered man and the new Earl, rode to Stirling with 600 men and beat up the town.

They sacked houses, roughed up the terrified townspeople, exhibited in public the letter of safe conduct and dragged it through Stirling attached to a horse's tail.

It was open defiance of the King of Scots.

They burned houses, and plundered.

James Douglas also put the King "to the horn", a grave insult. In Scotland at that time when a person refused to obey the law a horn was blown three times at the town cross and that meant the person was now an outlaw.

The Douglases were in fact saying that they considered the King to be King no longer.

The king's throne, reputation and effectiveness were in grave danger.

It is said that the King was so overcome with horror that he spoke of giving up the struggle against the nobles and of flying as a refugee to France.

But his friends reminded him of the old tale of the sheaf of arrows—unbreakable when they were tied together. Easily broken one by one. So the King resolved to deal with the other nobles on that basis.

He set out to re-establish himself. He had marched north with an army against the Earl of Crawford, and found he had already been defeated by the Earl of Huntly.

'In a rage - the King drew a knife

On June 12, 1452, in Parliament at Edinburgh the King was cleared of giving Douglas safe conduct. Parliament felt Douglas' traitorous refusal to name the bond justified his death and was guilty of his own death "by refusing the King's gentle persuasion."

The King was absolved of breach of faith, and the Douglas was declared to have been justly put to death.

Meanwhile, the Douglases were still, literally, up in arms. They posted letters of defiance on the doors of Parliament Hall.

But royal retribution was again to fall on them.

The King conferred favours and titles on the nobles and Church men who had supported him, and ensured their support.

He headed south with an army of 30,000 men and laid waste to the Douglas lands of Peebles, Selkirk and Dumfries.

Ultimately, James, the new Earl of Douglas, submitted to the King.

The King then turned his attention to the north. The Earl of Crawford submitted and terms were made with Ross as well.

The formidable alliance of the three earls ended.

All now seemed calm with the King again in the ascendency.

But the Douglases still simmered, and King James's spies again told him that the new Earl of Douglas was scheming and intriguing against the throne.

James resolved to crush them once and for all.

In March, 1455, he marched south again, burned crops and buildings, captured and sacked castles. Douglases' three brothers were defeated.

The key leaders had their heads cut off.

When Parliament again met on June 9, 1455, Douglas, his mother, the Countess Beatrice, and three brothers were all attainted and their estates forfeited.

Parliament then passed sweeping acts effectively giving the king the right to all key castles.

He took the lands of Douglas, Crawford and Ross, and was virtually an unchallenged monarch. The weak boy-King had become strong, warlike and clever, and he survived in an age of turbulence and intrigue.

His death, not surprisingly, was in war.

He was killed in 1460 when a cannon exploded at the seige of Roxburgh during the wars against the English. He was 29.

You can still see the room in Stirling Castle today where James II stabbed the Douglas.

The buildings overlooking the lawn do not contain the chamber where the Earl supped with the King: fire destroyed many apartments in later years.

But a small room where the stabbing took place survived.

It is sited above an old archway, and the window still exists through which the bloodcovered body was hurled after 'Fiery Face' lost his temper.

## THE SECRETS OF KING JAMES V

From the battlements of Stirling Castle you can see blue hills, green fields and woods, the silver links of the River Forth and many towns, villages and farms.

If you wonder what kind of people live there, how they earn their living and what they are really like, you will be following the thought processes of a Scottish monarch many centuries ago.

It is said that James V became so wearied of the life of the court, of the flatteries of men and women out for self-advancement, of the restrictions of protocol and formal behaviour that he rebelled.

He wanted to really know what his people were like. So he decided to find out.

He slipped out of the castle by day and by night in disguise and explored the town and countryside.

He was a daring person, and had been brought up in a hard school.

James V was born in Linlithgow in 1513 and was brought at an early age to Stirling.

He spent much of his early life in Edinburgh Castle but Stirling was his favourite.

His father had fallen with the flower of Scottish chivalry at the disastrous battle of Flodden, and James V came to the throne as a two-year-old boy in troubled times.

Scotland was beset by power-struggles among the great families and with intermittent war against England.

One of the branches of the famed Douglas family, the Red Douglases, virtually ruled the country for a time and kept the young King a prisoner.

They treated him so harshly that he never forgot it, and he determined to break their power.

He planned a daring escape.

*'The King and his servants gallop to the safety of Stirling Castle'*

When at Falkland Palace he told the Douglases he would be going hunting the next morning and that he wanted to go to bed early.

In the middle of the night, he slipped on his clothes, crept out to the stable, and silently obtained three horses for himself and two personal servants.

Then they galloped for their lives to the safety of Stirling Castle.

It was not surprising a King that could so look after himself could devise a plan to wander the countryside and get to know the people.

As a grown man, he talked with farmers, herdsmen, hunters and packmen and their wives. They did not know who he was. He pretended to be a minor laird and enjoyed himself sharing the customs and the hospitality of his subjects.

He got on well with people. The records of the time say he was not tall, but he was strong. He had a sharp wit, courteous manners, ate sparely and seldom drank wine. He had red hair, and the people called him the "Red Tod" or the "Red Fox".

It was said he could withstand cold, heat and hunger with a good humour, and that one of his main faults was a tendency towards romance and amours, a fairly common vice of the time.

It was also said that he was considerate, and ensured that any children of his liaisons were well cared for and their mothers given financial aid.

The King was also fond of music and poetry and records show accounts-entries for lutes, and lute strings, for viols and repairs to an organ.

He had been greatly influenced as a youth by Sir David Lyndsay of the Mount, Lord Lyon King-at-Arms, a poet of great repute in his day.

He was an enthusiastic patron of the popular Mayday pastimes and games, attended plays and festivals and won and gave prizes for archery and wrestling.

He enjoyed field sports, and had a passion for horses.

It was little wonder the people respected him and gave him the affectionate title of "King of the Commons".

James V planned his incognito journeyings with great care.

He gave himself the title of "Gudeman of Ballengeich" from the steep path leading to the main town, on the north-west side of the castle, where the present Ballengeich road is now situated. It separates the castle from the Gowan Hill.

The ancient gateway to the castle, erected by Robert II and now built-up, was sited there.

The name means the stormy or windy pass, and was probably originally written as Ballochgiech. Gudeman was a description

*'James won prizes for wrestling'*

applied to a class of small proprietors who held their land, not from the crown, but from a vassal.

It was a wise choice by the King. Enough rank to explain his bearing and manners. Not too high to discourage friendly and intimate relationships with the common people.

The incidents of his wanderings became the subject of many a legend, and were told in ballad and song, such as "The Gaberlunzie Man" and "We'll Gang Nae Mair A-Roving".

He did not always travel for the purposes of gallantry or the love of personal adventure.

There are stories of him dealing out summary justice to known wrongdoers, and of attacking bandits either single-handed or with a few attendants.

Sir Walter Scott drew on fact in his epic poem "The Lady of the Lake" when he described the famous single combat fight between the King as Fitzjames and the Highland chieftain, Rhoderick Dhu.

Once when the King was out hunting he was separated from his attendants and entered a cottage in the middle of a moor not far from the foot of the Ochil Hills. He was not recognised and was kindly received.

The farmer told his wife to fetch the hen that roosted nearest the cock, which is always the plumpest, for the stranger's supper.

The King was highly pleased with his food and the company and told his host that he would return his kindness. He told the farmer that when he next came to Stirling he should call at the castle and ask for the Gudeman of Ballengeich.

He did so, and was astounded to discover that he had entertained the King.

In front of laughing courtiers, the King entertained him...and then lightheartedly gave him the title King of the Moors.

Legend has it that the King visited a miller's house near Falkland, and got on so well that he jokingly asked the miller whether he would like the fourth part, the eighth or the sixteenth part of the lands on which they stood.

The miller is said to have lightheartedly replied that the sixteenth was over greedy, the fourth part would be cheating himself and he would strike between the two and ask for nothing.

Laughing, the King identified himself...and gave him the eighth part.

Although he could be tough with serious wrongdoers, he could take a joke, as the modern saying has it.

# THE SECRETS OF KING JAMES V

Carriers taking royal goods to Stirling took a route which passed the house of Buchanan of Arnprior.

The laird who could be a law unto himself, asked one of the carriers to dump his load and he would pay him for it.

The carrier refused, telling him that his goods were for the King.

Buchanan then took the goods by force.

"If King James is King of Scotland then I am King of Kippen," he said. It was reasonable, he said that the King should share his goods with his neighbour-king.

The alarmed and empty-handed carrier fled to the castle and complained to the king's servants, who informed James.

Off set the angry King for Kippen, accompanied by a few retainers.

He demanded access to Buchanan's house, but was refused by a man carrying a battleaxe who said there could be no access until dinner was over.

The King asked again, and got another blunt refusal.

Then he told the man to tell his master that the Gudeman of Ballengeich desired to speak with the King of Kippen.

Out came Buchanan of Arnprior and was astounded to recognise his sovereign.

Both men laughed. The King entered, and Buchanan entertained him so well that they became firm friends and the King gave him leave to take what he wanted when the royal carts were passing his door.

Buchanan was asked to the castle, and to the enjoyment of all was treated as the King of Kippen.

There is another story that when the King was residing at Holyrood Palace he was attacked by four or five footpads when returning from one of his private jaunts.

He took a stance on a high and narrow bridge over the River Almond and defended himself with a light sword.

A peasant, threshing in a nearby farm, heard the noise and joined what he thought was the weaker man. He laid about with a flail, and the robbers fled.

He invited James into his barn where the King asked for a basin and towel.

The King found out through casual conversation that his new friend's dearest earthly wish was to possess his farm upon which he worked as a bondsman.

The lands belonged to the Crown.

James did not tell him who he was, but invited the man to come to Holyrood and ask for the Gudeman of Ballengeich.

The man eventually came...

The King revealed himself.

He presented his helper with the farm lands under the service of presenting an ewer, basin and towel for the King to wash his hands when he should happen to pass the Bridge of Cramond.

The stories of the wandering king, romantic, hardy, good-humoured and at ease with all people, lasted for centuries.

He had not had an easy life, and he did not succeed in achieving his national wishes for himself or his people.

There were too many major difficulties facing him, resolute though he was.

As an adult, he had plenty of trouble on his hands. He said Scotland was not big enough to hold him and the Douglases and he initially restricted their area of influence.

They were not to come within six miles of him. Then he had their estates seized, and banished them from the country.

He did his best to bring law-and-order to the unruly Border country, including the summary hanging of the head of the powerful Armstrong family.

He dealt with the Clan chiefs in the Highlands in the same way—making friends with some, punishing others.

He had constant friction with Henry VIII over his war with France and the mammoth events of the Reformation.

James was determined for political and religious reasons to stay friendly with France, and in 1536 he married Madelaine, daughter of King Francis I, with that aim in mind.

Sadly, she died not long afterwards. Henry VIII was infuriated once more when two years later James married another French-woman, Mary of Lorraine, who became the mother of Mary, Queen of Scots.

War broke out between Scotland and England, and because of disorganisation, quarrels over leadership and lack of planning the Scots were easily routed by a smaller English army at the battle of Solway Moss.

These events broke James' health and nerve. His only two lawful children died, and he took himself to Falkland Palace where he died in 1542 shortly after hearing that a daughter had been born to him, the future and ill-fated Mary Queen of Scots.

He is said to have uttered the oft-quoted words: "It cam' wi' a lass, and it will gang wi' a lass", meaning that the crown that had come to the Stewarts by a woman, Marjorie Bruce, daughter of King Robert I, would be lost through the girl that had just been born.

Poor James! He felt his life had been a failure.

Yet there are lasting memorials to him. He set up the Court of Session in Edinburgh, Scotland's greatest civil law court, which operates to this day.

And in Stirling Castle there are stories in stone, the great palace that he built and a statue at the corner of the wall next to the Great Hall.

The Palace windows are surmounted by stones showing I 5 for James V.

The figure at the corner is thought to show the King disguised as the Gudeman o' Ballengeich.

The "King of the Commons" is not forgotten either in legend or amid the mementoes of history.

# THE MIGHTY SHIP OF STIRLING CASTLE.

There was tremendous excitement in the castle and the town. Torches flared. Trumpets blew. Messengers clattered off on horse-back. The townspeople poured out of the houses to see what the fuss was about.

They told one another of the great news.

A son had been born to the King.

It meant a great deal because James VI was now 28 and the continuance of the Scottish crown in the house of Stewart had seemed a precarious thing.

The King and his Queen, Anne of Denmark, rejoiced that February day in 1593-4.

The baby was to become Henry, Prince and Steward of Scotland and Duke of Rothesay. He was also created in 1610, Prince of Wales, but sadly he did not live to succeed to the crowns of Scotland and England. He died aged 18 not long after James had become King of England as well as Scotland.

Still, at the time of the birth, hopes ran high for a glorious future.

It was no surprise when the king and queen decided to make the baptism of Prince Henry a great occasion.

Their celebration became the talk of European courts.

Preparations began months ahead. Royalty from other lands and ambassadors were invited to attend.

Large sums were spent on their accommodation and entertainment. The King built the Chapel Royal in Stirling Castle specifically for the baptism, replacing an earlier chapel in bad repair.

Scotland wanted to do the occasion justice.

As with a major royal occasion today, no expense was spared. Every co-operation from townspeople was expected to ensure that all went well on the day.

All the leading Scottish nobles were asked to attend and any who did not were in disfavour for a long time to come.

The King wanted a peaceful and joyful celebration, but there were problems. Rivalries between great families, clans and houses could easily lead to quarrels and blows with so many retainers and soldiers flocking around castle and town, each eager to demonstrate his own master's importance and recalling old feuds.

The King issued a special proclamation. It was read at the Mercat Cross of Stirling on August 24. Three heralds and two trumpeters took part to emphasise its importance.

The message was unmistakable. No matter the rank, high or low, the king expected no brawling. He demanded good behaviour, courtesy to the visiting ambassadors and their retainers, and urged that the nobles should select servants who were well-behaved.

All this should be done for the good name of Scotland.

The baptism was delayed for some days because the Queen of England's special envoy was ill and his replacement was held up by bad weather.

When it did take place there was much to marvel at. There were tournaments which delighted the crowds, and a splendid banquet.

Rooms were hung with velvet and taffeta or cloth-of-gold. Rich presents were given, and honours bestowed.

But it was the events which were to take place inside the Great Hall of Stirling Castle which were to set the tongues wagging.

A huge gathering sat down to the banquet, with the King, the Queen and ambassadors at a top table. All could see down the middle of the hall.

Great care had been taken with seating arrangements. A lady of high rank was seated between each noble and overseas visitor.

After the first course the trumpets played a fanfare, and there was then appreciative murmuring from the guests.

The second course, a dessert, was carried in on a table placed on a chariot twelve feet long and seven broad.

The chariot was moved by men hidden within it and screened from the guests by hanging cloths. It was led by a blackamoor dressed in rich clothes and wearing a harness of pure gold.

It was accompanied by six ladies, three in white satin and three in crimson, with feathers and jewels on their heads. Each lady carried a badge to denote her identity, plus a motto.

They represented Ceres, the goddess of agriculture and civilisation, and such themes as Fecundity, Faith, Concord, Liberality and Perseverance.

They served the dessert to the guests, and then they and the chariot left the hall, amid applause.

The King had originally intended to have the chariot drawn by a real lion which had been brought specially from Holyroodhouse, but the idea was dropped, possibly because of the danger to the guests.

But more was to follow.

'The proclamation was read at the Merkat Cross'

The third course was of fish, crabs, lobster and shellfish made with sugar and brought in a way that led to cheers, clapping and gasps of amusement.

An immense "ship" appeared from behind screens to another fanfare of trumpets.

It was 18 feet long, eight feet wide, and forty feet high to the top of the masts and flags.

It was mounted on a wheeled base designed to depict the sea, and weighed several tons.

A lady stood at her helm, wearing cloth of gold, and appeared to guide the ship.

Many men were hidden inside heaving at levers and wheels. Over 30 people crowded her decks, waving to the guests and performing seamanlike tasks.

The pilot and five seamen wore special Spanish taffeta, fourteen musicians wore the royal colours of red-and-gold, and mythical and nautical characters—well-known to the people of that time—were depicted.

Arion with his harp who, myth said, had been rescued from the sea by dolphins. Neptune, God of the Sea, was there with his trident. So was Thetis, mother of Achilles, with her mace and Triton and the son of Neptune, with his trumpet.

Neptune wore an Indian cloth of silver and silk, and the rest were also richly dressed.

The ship was also accompanied by other characters of the sea, ladies and girls dressed as sirens and mermaids.

They wore pearls, coral, shells and precious metals.

In addition to this colourful and laughing crew, which received rapturous applause from the guests, the ship also had 36 brass guns.

There were political lessons for the guests.

The ship commemorated the King's voyage across the North Sea to fetch his bride from Scandinavia.

Latin mottoes painted on the sails of white taffeta, or carried by the crew, helped emphasise the point.

The royal colours added further weight.

The masts were painted red. The rigging was of red silk, the blocks of gold and the anchors silver-gilt.

The mainsail bore the arms of Scotland and Denmark and another sail bore the emblem of the North Star.

The trumpets blared again. There was more applause as the ship hoisted its sails and creaked its way up the hall to the top table.

Then shouts of surprise and some alarm. A salute was fired from some of the guns which made many of the guests jump.

*'An immense ship appeared'*

The musicians played with renewed vigour and the mermaids sang, and the audience quietened down again.

The ship 'sailed' to the high table, halted and dropped its anchor.

More music followed. Arion, dressed like a dolphin, played his harp. There was more singing.

The audience watched enraptured as Neptune supervised the unloading of the sugar-objects cargo.

There was more appreciative murmuring when it was seen that the food being carried was in beautifully fashioned and ornamented glasses.

The musicians continued to sing and play, and the whole crew sang a hymn of congratulations to the king, queen and prince.

More music followed, including an appropriate psalm.

The departure of the ship was equally impressive. The anchor was raised, trumpets sounded, and the ship moved in stately fashion down the hall, while within her hidden and sweating workmen toiled again at their wheels and levers.

Just before she vanished behind the screens she fired all her remaining guns.

The fun was not yet over because the royal party and the guests adjourned to another hall to continue feasting until the early hours of the morning.

Special displays of this kind were not unknown at the time, but the Stirling ship was in a class of its own.

Reports tell of marvelling guests, and tales went back to many places in Europe of the Scottish skills in design and craftsmanship that had brought it about.

The English ambassadors did not mention it in their reports, possibly—some historians think—because they did not wish to arouse Queen Elizabeth's envy.

The ship was later stripped of its rich hangings and furnishings and it went into store.

It was never used again, but later reports tell of it being in Stirling Castle nearly two centuries later.

Its memory stayed for a long time.

Envoys and nobles, and the townspeople who heard of it from servants and workmen who had for many weeks and months built it and furnished it, felt deep pride that the Scottish court could put on such a show.

After that, the ship vanished, and no trace now remains of one of the castle's great events.

# LAST SHOTS IN ANGER

It used to be said that some of the older houses near Stirling Castle had nicks and gashes in the stonework, a relic of the days when shots were last fired in anger from the battlements.

It was not all that long ago. It happened when Prince Charles Edward Stuart's Jacobite army was retreating northwards towards the end of the 1745-46 Rising.

They had been in the vicinity before. When they marched south the previous September after the Prince had raised his Standard at Glenfinnan, in the West Highlands, they had passed within cannon shot of the castle.

The Clansmen had then marched in good order, with colours flying and pipes playing.

The Hanoverian garrison had fired several shots, most of which fell short or passed harmlessly over. The Highlanders had jeered, and continued their triumphant march to Edinburgh, and their victory at Prestonpans.

But now in the bleak weather of January all was different. A new grimness was in the air. The Prince's army, en route to London, had decided to turn at Derby, a move hotly argued about to this day. London was in turmoil and it was possible that had the Highlanders kept going that they would have won all and re-established the Stuarts on the throne of Britain.

But the decision was taken to return to Scotland, to see the winter out, to try and capture the Hanoverian forts in the Highlands and then, when spring came, to burst out anew with a larger army drawn from the Clans sympathetic to the Stuart cause.

Many Stirling townspeople were opposed to the Prince, and a 400 strong militia was formed and given muskets and swords by the castle garrison.

General Blakeney, who commanded the castle, energetically put his defences in order. He blew up the southern arch of Stirling Bridge to prevent the Jacobites crossing.

The Prince hoped to capture the castle and established his headquarters at Bannockburn. He sent his best general, Lord George Murray, to Alloa to meet with Lord John Drummond who several days before had landed in the north-east with heavy artillery and stores from France, necessary if the Jacobites were to capture the Highland forts.

On January 4, 1746, the Prince's army occupied the outskirts of Stirling and the next day he sent a letter to the town council, with a drummer boy, ordering the town to surrender.

The militia, unused to the niceties of war protocol, fired on the boy and he ran away, leaving his drum.

A second letter was sent warning the town of dire consequences, and it surrendered on January 8.

The castle garrison continued to defy the prince.

There was much acrimony and recrimination later about the surrender. Those who wanted to fight said they had the support of the castle soldiers. Those who had counselled surrender argued that they had no strong defences, only slight dykes or hedges on some sides of the town, and the Prince had a battery of smaller cannon and larger cannon across the Forth. The town had no cannon at all.

The question of whether the Prince got his larger cannon or not from Alloa across the Forth was crucial to the fate of the castle.

The Hanoverian troops did what they could. They had broken the bridge, and they stationed sloops offshore at Alloa to prevent a crossing of the Forth there. General Henry Hawley, who was pursuing the Jacobites north, sent small boats and 300 men from Leith, including one with a small cannon, to attack the Jacobites on the shores of the Forth and to try to dislodge them.

It was a difficult job for the Prince's army to move their cannon, because they included heavy pieces: two 16-pounders, two 12-pounders and two eight-pounders.

There was skirmishing along the banks of the Forth, including a vigorous clash at Airth, and the Jacobites eventually sent their light cannon up to the Fords of Frew, an ancient crossing in the carseland about six miles from Stirling. Lord George Murray speedily brought men from Falkirk, where his main army was based, and set up four guns to command the south shore of the Forth.

The heavier cannons were loaded on a captured ship at Alloa.

*'As castle garrison fired shots - the Highlanders jeered'*

The Jacobites bombarded the Hanoverian sloops from the shore and cut their cables, and they drifted down river on the tide.

The way was clear, but there were still difficulties. One cannon alone weighed 1¾ tons and needed 20 horses to pull it.

Eventually all were brought near to the castle where General Blakeney's men kept watch and got ready to withstand the now-certain bombardment.

But trouble was to befall the Jacobite army.

The Prince was advised on artillery matters by two men, one a Scot, James Alexander Grant, and the other a Frenchman, Mirabelle de Gordon.

The second man was a French engineer, a Chevalier of the Order of St. Louis, and he had been sent to Scotland with Lord John Drummond. He was treated as a gunnery expert but his experience was limited.

Mr. Grant wanted trenches dug and the guns established on ground at the side of the town, opposite the castle gate and beside the present cemetery and Holy Rude Church. It was a good position, reasonably well sheltered and within easy range.

The alarmed inhabitants protested that the site was too near dwelling houses. Monsignor Mirabelle's view then prevailed.

He had trenches dug on the Gowan Hill, to the north of the castle, where there was only 15 inches of earth above solid rock. The exposed Jacobite gunners had to build barricades and shelters from bags of wool and sacks filled with earth.

They were quickly blasted out of their badly-chosen and ill-protected gun positions, and were forced to build higher and stronger barricades.

Reports speak of them losing 25 men a day.

When the Prince called on the castle to surrender, General Blakeney refused with good reason. The garrison were standing firm and were as yet in no real peril.

By January 15 little progress had been made.

By this time the Prince had a major battle on his hands because General Hawley with a Hanoverian army was nearing Falkirk, and it was clear the Highlanders would have to fight this determined and tough opponent.

The Prince was not short of men at this stage. He had at least 1200 disposed at the castle and in Stirling and almost 10,000 at Falkirk.

Thanks to brilliant generalship by Lord George Murray, the Highlanders fought—other than one indisciplined charge—a brave and controlled engagement and swept Hawley's army from the field, capturing much equipment and many prisoners including the hangman which General Hawley had brought with him to execute Jacobites should they be defeated.

The Prince and his leaders discussed whether they should pursue General Hawley's fleeing army or continue the siege of Stirling Castle.

Mirabelle de Gordon advised them that the castle would surrender in a day or so, and the harassed Jacobite gunners had more trenches dug on the Gowan Hill and more barricades built.

They managed to get three of their seven battering cannon in place.

On January 29 the cannons belched smoke and the crashing echoes reverberated around the town.

The balls crashed into the castle walls, sending up showers of masonry and stones and causing serious damage.

It began to look as if a breach would be made.

But General Blakeney quickly replied with his nine-pounders and dismounted the Jacobite guns and demolished most of their emplacements. Several of the Jacobite officers were deeply angered for they had advised that Mirabelle should not open fire until all seven guns were ready.

There were many dead, and fierce quarrels broke out with Mirabelle.

As time passed men began to slip away from the Jacobite army, to take booty home, or to see to wife and family, and their cattle and small fields, but it was not desertion in the modern sense.

It was understood they would return when they could, and certainly in the spring.

The chiefs advised Prince Charles to retreat into the Highlands. His army, they said, was not strong enough to stand another lowland engagement at the moment. They should try and take the Highland forts and re-muster in the spring.

Eventually and sadly, the order was given for a retreat into the northern hills and glens.

It was an untidy retreat, so unlike the confident march south when the flags flew and the pipes played and the men cheered and jeered at the castle troops.

The Clansmen straggled north by bands. The baggage carts and cannon were spiked and abandoned.

An ammunition dump at St. Ninians Church accidentally blew up and two local people were killed. Only the steeple was left. It can still be seen to this day.

The main force marched to Dunblane by the Fords of Frew, and then to the north.

'An ammunition Dump at St. Ninian's church blew up'

From the battlements of Stirling Castle the soldiers of General Blakeney watched them go, and fired a few rounds in derision...the last shots in anger ever to be fired from Stirling Castle.

They saw the red and green tartans of the Stewarts and Macdonalds, the Camerons and the MacGregors, the McLarens, Farquharsons, Robertsons, the McGillivrays, the Macintoshes, and the other Clans who followed the Prince disappear into the distance.

They were also disappearing into history because it was to be the last time that a Stirling Castle garrison would see such an army on the march.

On the same day as the Jacobites left, the advance guard of General (Butcher) Cumberland entered the town. The castle guns fired once more, but this time in salute.

The old bridge of Stirling was repaired, and the Hanoverian army left for the north and ultimately for the battlefield of Culloden where the hopes of the House of Stuart were to be dashed for ever.

The shots fired at Stirling signalled the beginning of the end of the Gaelic and Highland way of life. They marked a new turn in the train of events that eventually led to the suppression of the tartan, of the power of the chiefs, to the complex factors which brought sweeping changes in Highland life and ultimately led to the Clearances, the emptying of the glens and mass emigration.

Stirling was so often the focal point of so much that was significant in Scottish wars.

The gun-duel between General Blakeney's soldiers and the Jacobite artillerymen on the Gowan Hill was, in its own way, one of the turning points of the final Jacobite rising.

So, if you see scores and marks on old buildings or are lucky enough to find a musket or cannon ball buried in ground roundabout it will be a final memento of the last time guns were fired from the battlements of Stirling Castle, and the last time a beseiging army set out to capture this ancient fortress.

# DEAD MEN'S VIEW

Stirling Castle has many memories. Some are humorous, some gruesome and some are odd and puzzling.

As you walk round the battlements have a good look down to the ground below...and you will wonder how John Damien only suffered a broken leg after he dived off the edge in a vain bid to fly.

The exact spot is unknown but it is thought to be somewhere near the garden parapet.

It all happened in 1507, in the reign of King James IV.

John Damien, a Frenchman, was what today we would call an amateur scientist and what people then called an apothecary.

He wormed his way into the King's favour, and among other experiments he attempted to turn base metals into gold.

The King was initially impressed and appointed him Abbot of Tungland, in Galloway, as a reward for his labours.

Others were not so receptive and referred to him sarcastically as the "French leech", a reference both to his alleged medical skills and his attachment to the King.

After a time, King James grew disenchanted with him and Damien, alarmed at his waning popularity, endeavoured to get back into favour.

He announced that he had made a pair of wings, and that he intended to fly off the castle walls and that he would be in France before the King's ambassadors could get there.

This plan was greeted with great excitement and some scepticism.

A large crowd of nobles, retainers, soldiers and servants gathered at the battlements and, as the word spread, a mob of townspeople gathered at the bottom, warily looking upwards.

John Damien strapped on his large wings, made of light wood to which were attached many feathers from eagles wings, plus some from the wings of hens.

He stepped on to the edge of the battlements, and a hush fell.

Then he sprang into the air and jumped off.

There were cries of consternation as he plummeted downwards, arms flailing, and thudded into the ground.

The people below began to jeer as Damien was carried away.

He had been fortunate in escaping with only a fractured leg. Some reports say he broke his thigh bone.

Damien blamed the accident on the fact that he had used some hens' feathers in the wings. They had coveted the midden, and not the skies, he said.

The Scottish poet William Dunbar wrote a satirical poem about the event called "The Ballad of the Fenzeit Freir of Tungland".

Damien was said to be more deeply hurt by the mob's jeers and the ridicule of the court than the pain of his leg, but the story had a happy ending for him—the King was so taken by the amusement of the bizarre experiment and, possibly, by Damien's courage that he received him at court once more.

Odd happenings?

Well, in the reign of Robert III a strange, wearied, stranger called Thomas Warde of Trumpington turned up at the castle.

He bore the marks of imprisonment and privation, and looked exactly like King Richard II of England.

He had appeared at the court of the Lord of the Isles, at Islay, and was produced at Stirling as a person likely to be of advantage in time of strife with England.

King Richard's end was obscure and many people in Scotland and England thought he had escaped from prison.

Quite what the Scots hoped to get from the stranger is not clear, but for a long time a so-called King of England, known in history as the "Mammet" or the false King, lived in Stirling Castle. He died there in 1419.

He was not the only 'pretender' to visit Stirling.

King James IV received in 1495 the imposter, Perkin Warbeck, and he was treated with great courtesy as the reputed son of Edward IV of England.

The Scottish nobles followed their monarch's example, and the Earl of Huntly even agreed to a marriage with his daughter.

Perkin Warbeck was given a large pension, and James made war on England on his behalf in 1496 and again the next year.

But the deception could not last for ever and relationships between Perkin Warbeck and the King became strained.

Perkin Warbeck eventually left Scotland for the south in 1497.

Gruesome tales? There are any number.

Take a walk to the Gowan Hills, where the two cannon from Napoleonic times sit beside the spot where people were beheaded in past centuries.

Look all round at the lovely hills, fields and woods. It must have been heart-breaking for many a man to kneel, or stand, hands bound, and look at that view and know that within a few minutes the swish and thud of the executioner's axe would shut his eyes for ever.

There are arguments over the meaning of the name Gowan Hills, but one theory is that it is from a Scots word for lamentation.

It was here King James I had some of Scotland's leading nobles executed.

He was a man of firm resolve, and determined to curb lawlessness in the country, whether it was by warring nobles or by common robbers and thieves.

In 1424 he had returned to his native land 18 years after being captured as a boy by the English when on his way to France.

On his return, he uttered the famous words: "If God grants me life, I will make the key keep the castle and the bracken-bush the cow".

In other words, the laws of the realm were to be obeyed by all.

A year after his coronation at Scone King James held court at Stirling Castle in May, 1425, and drastic measures followed.

He had little love for his cousin, the Regent Murdoch, Duke of Albany, or his family, for they had kept his father and grandfather from ruling, and had control of Scotland when he was prisoner in England.

The King also probably believed that the Albany family were responsible for starving his brother, David, to death, and that they may have prolonged his imprisonment by the English in the hope of taking the throne.

The King also feared their power and perhaps he had cast covetous eyes at their large estates.

But whatever the reason, or mixture of reasons, the outcome was swift and straightforward.

He jailed Duke Murdoch's eldest son, Walter Stewart, on a charge of robbery, and followed that up by imprisoning Duncan, Earl of Lennox, the father of Duke Murdoch's wife.

*'Damien plummeted downwards'*

For good measure, he then imprisoned Duke Murdoch himself, his wife and another son.

Not surprisingly, there were repercussions and another of the Duke's sons gathered a small army, attacked the town of Dumbarton, killed townspeople, burned houses and slew the Keeper of Dumbarton Castle.

Duke Murdoch, his two sons, and the Earl of Lennox were summarily tried by the King.

They were brought to the Heading Hill on the Gowan Hills and beheaded.

Tales abounded in Scotland of the King's severity and determination.

After dealing with the Albany family he turned his attention to the powerful and unruly clan chiefs of the Highlands and Islands.

He summoned them to a parliament at Inverness, and when they attended—including Alexander, Lord of the Isles—James immediately ordered the arrest of the 40 leading chiefs. He jailed most of them, and had the most dangerous executed.

Inevitably, he made implacable enemies.

The Gowan Hills at Stirling were to figure in a horrible way in an event not long after the King's death.

He had incurred the hatred of Sir Robert Graham, whom he had jailed for a time, and he had also taken Graham lands.

The Grahams and other nobles who hated the King plotted to kill him.

Then followed the well-known story of James' assassination in the Blackfriars Monastery at Perth where he went to spend Christmas in 1436.

The King's chamberlain, Sir Robert Stewart, the Master of Atholl, betrayed him, laid planks across the monastery moat and ensured the door-locks would not fasten.

When the King heard the noise of the band of would-be murderers trying to get in, he quickly tore up the floorboards and hid in a vault below.

One of the ladies with him, Katherine Douglas, is said to have put her arm through the staples of the room-door to prevent Graham's band bursting in, but to no avail. Ultimately, the King was discovered, and stabbed to death.

There was a cruel sequel.

The Queen—and the King's great love—was Lady Joan Beaufort, daughter of the Earl of Somerset. He had fallen in love with her when he was in England, and wrote beautiful poetry about her, and called her his "milk-white dove".

She was grief-stricken at James' murder, and vowed never to rest until the killers were caught.

Their end was terrible. The conspirators were tortured for three days. Graham was nailed naked to a tree and dragged through the streets. He was tortured with red-hot pincers. His son was also tortured in front of him and then executed on the Heading Hill of the Gowan Hills.

Atholl—thought to be plotting to succeed to the throne—had a crown of red-hot metal placed on his head and was not executed at the Heading Hill, but died after torture.

Eventually, Graham, too, had his agonies ended by the headsman's axe.

Violent days!

There are light-hearted memories, too, of the Gowan Hills.

One section, at the north end, was known as Hurly-Hawky, well-known as the site of a sliding game, using the skeleton of a cow's head as a kind of sledge.

The name is said to derive from the words *hurl*, to move rapidly, and *hawky*, a name for a cow.

King James V—the "Gudeman of Ballengeich"—is believed to have taken part in this amusement, sometimes repeated today by children using pieces of old carpet or linoleum as sledges.